Aero and Officer Mike

POLICE PARTNERS

Aero and Officer Mike

POLICE PARTNERS

by Joan Plummer Russell

Photographs by Kris Turner Sinnenberg

BOYDS MILLS PRESS

Acknowledgments

I would like to thank Shaker Heights Police Chief Walter A. Ugrinic, who gave me permission to share a K-9's view from a cruiser; Mayor Patricia Mearns, an Aero fan; Commander Michael Gale; Sheryl Benford, Director of Law; Lisa Gale, Chief Prosecutor; Lieutenant James Mariano; Sergeant John Danko; Rosemary Price; Corporal Norwood Richmond; and other Shaker Heights Police Department officers and personnel who graciously helped in different ways. A special thank-you to K-9 handlers Corporal Tim Keck with Argus and Officer Jaime Planinsek with Ben, who so often smoothed the way behind the scenes; also to northeast Ohio K-9 handlers, who welcomed me on many of their training days; and to Shaker Heights Fire Department; Evan Morse, D.V.M.; Reverend Martin Amos; and especially to Karen Klockner, who gave me a wonderful birthday gift, her offer to be my editor.
—J.P.R.

Thanks to Officer Mike for opening up his job to the scrutiny of a camera. Going behind the scenes with him and his impressive dog was pure fun. Thanks to my husband for being understanding; also to Dodd Camera & Imaging; Drug Certification participants, including Corporal Tim Keck, Officer Jaime Planinsek, and K-9 Ben; editor Karen Klockner; Lieutenant Jim Mariano; Lieutenant Mike Schwarber; MotoPhoto Portrait Studio of Shaker Heights; The Nature Center at Shaker Lakes; Officer Steve Tajgiszer; photographer Tim Turner of Chicago; Sergeant Bob Doles; Shaker Heights Citizens Police Academy Commanders Sergeant John Danko and Patrolman Vince Kovacic; Shaker Heights Fire Department; Shaker Heights Police Chief Walter Ugrinic; Special Weapons and Tactics of the Shaker Heights Police Department; Rhonda Hegyes Stefanski; and University School.
Sadly, two northeast Ohio police dogs died while this book was being photographed:
Argus, of cancer, and Cero, in the line of duty.
Finally, thanks to friends who imagine the possibilities.
—K.T.S.

Published by Caroline House
Boyds Mills Press, Inc.
A Highlights Company
815 Church Street
Honesdale, Pennsylvania 18431
Printed in China

U.S. Cataloging-in-Publication Data
(Library of Congress Standards)

Russell, Joan Plummer.
Aero and Officer Mike: police partners / by Joan Plummer Russell ;
photographs by Kris Turner Sinnenberg. —1st ed.
[32]p. : col. ill. ; cm.
Summary: A photo essay about police dogs at work and play.
ISBN 1-56397-931-4
1. Police Dogs. 2. Dogs. I. Sinnenberg, Kris Turner. II. Title.
363.2/ 32 21 2001 CIP AC
00-105775

First edition, 2001
Book design by Amy Drinker, Aster Designs
The text of this book is set in 15.5-point Minion book.

10 9 8 7 6 5 4 3 2 1

To Bob, at last!
To all my family members, who were constant cheerleaders.
To Corporal Michael E. Matsik, who shared his cruiser for many hours
each month and patiently answered my thousands of questions.
To all brave K-9 handlers and their well-trained,
magnificent K-9s all over the country.
And to K.J., Lori, Megan, and Shane.

—J.P.R.

To my parents, who always advised me that
anything is possible if you really try.
And to my husband, kids, and pets, for putting life in perspective.

—K.T.S.

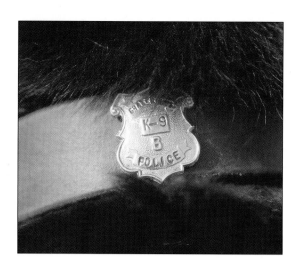

Aero

It is very early in the morning. Everyone in the house is still asleep. A large black-and-tan German shepherd is lying on the floor by Officer Mike's bed. The alarm rings. Officer Mike reaches down to pet his dog, Aero.

Aero is a police dog, also known as a K-9 officer. When Officer Mike puts on his uniform with a silver badge on his chest, Aero jumps up, ready to have his wide black leather collar with a police badge on it slipped over his head. He knows this will be a work day.

Officer Mike and Aero are partners. They work together. They practice together. They play together. They live with Officer Mike's wife and daughter, a cat named Tarzan, and a Chihuahua named Zeus.

Aero, with his powerful nose, can do many things Officer Mike cannot. He can sniff and find lost children. He can sniff and find lost things. He can sniff and find hidden drugs.

Police dogs are very strong and well trained. They have to be ready to go anywhere they are needed. They can be very fierce when they are helping to catch criminals. They can run faster than any human being. But when

work and

police dogs are
not working, they
are gentle pets that
like to have their
tummies scratched.
Aero's most

important jobs are to help and to protect his partner, Officer Mike.
Together, Aero and Officer Mike patrol in all kinds of weather. Some
weeks they patrol from early morning until dinnertime. Some weeks they
sleep in the daytime and work all night.

Aero is always eager to jump into the back of the police car. Officer Mike's car is different from other police cars. There is no back seat. The floor is flat and covered with carpet for Aero to lie on. There is a water bowl built into the floor, and a small fan keeps Aero cool in the summer. Screens cover the windows so no one can reach in and pet him.

When Aero is on duty, he's not allowed to play. Officer Mike sits in the driver's seat, but Aero will not let anyone else sit in the front until Officer Mike tells Aero it is OK.

Aero knows that one of his jobs is to protect the police car. When Officer Mike leaves the car, he either opens the front window for Aero to jump through or uses a remote control to open the back door when he needs Aero's help.

When it's time to begin a work shift, Officer Mike and Aero check in at the police station. There, emergency calls are being monitored in a communications center filled with computers, camera screens, telephones, and police radios.

Officer Mike and Aero start their patrol by driving slowly up and down the streets to see if everyone is safe. If a burglar alarm goes off at someone's house, a dispatcher calls Officer Mike on his radio and sends him to that address.

partners on

Officer Mike and Aero check all around the house to make sure there has not been a break-in. Sometimes it's a false alarm. They also may be called to a store if a robbery is taking place, or to help control large crowds and keep everyone safe. Whenever an officer answers a call, a second officer is always sent as backup.

patrol

time for

When Aero and Officer Mike have been in the police car for a few hours, Aero will need to take a break. Aero pushes his head against his partner's head to let him know. Officer Mike parks the cruiser as soon as he can and says to Aero, "Go be a dog!" Aero knows he'll also have time to explore a little and maybe chase a tennis ball while they are stopped.

a break

signals

Officer Mike can talk to Aero in different ways. One way is to use hand and arm signals. When Mike's hand is outstretched, it means "stay." When Mike's arm is raised, it means "sit." When his hand is flat, it means "down."

Aero is very loyal to Officer Mike and wants to obey him. He likes to hear the words "Good dog!" He tries to please his partner all the time.

and commands

Aero can understand short commands like "Find him!" or "Stop him!" and "No barking!" Aero can also understand some commands in Czech, the language spoken where he was born and where he began his training as a police dog. Czech sounds very different from English. *Sedni* means "sit." *Knoze* means "heel." And *lehni* means "down."

K-9 training

Aero's training never ends. Several times a month Aero and Officer Mike train with other officers and their K-9 partners. One exercise the police dogs do is to run through an obstacle course and practice getting over, under, around, and through difficult spots.

Aero had to learn how to walk up and down very steep, open stairs. He also had to learn to walk over a large, open grating, the kind you often see on city streets. At first he spread his paws to help keep his balance. His legs began to quiver, and he whined a frightened cry. He had to practice over and over. Officer Mike kept saying, "Good boy, you can do it." Aero was brave and trusted his partner, but he still does not like open gratings or steep stairs.

Aero practices catching and holding bad guys. This is a huge help to Officer Mike. When Aero is training, another officer will wear a thickly padded sleeve on his arm. Officer Mike will give the command, "Stop him!" Aero will swiftly run to the pretend bad guy and grab the padded sleeve in his mouth. The sleeve protects the officer's arm from Aero's teeth. This may seem like a great game for Aero, but it is also serious practice. In real life, the suspect would not have a padded sleeve. Aero would grab the person's arm and hold it with his teeth until Officer Mike could put on the handcuffs.

S.W.A.T.

Aero and Officer Mike are part of the S.W.A.T. team, a group of officers assigned to very dangerous work. S.W.A.T. stands for "Special Weapons and Tactics." The S.W.A.T. team is called when hostages are taken or at other times when a specially trained police team is needed. Aero sometimes has to sit alone for hours on watch until Mike calls for his help. He might have to lie completely still in the snow or rain or under the hot sun. He stays in one spot until Officer Mike gives a different command.

K-9s have very powerful noses—hundreds of times more powerful than human noses. That's why one of Aero's most helpful talents on the police force is his ability to find things by smell.

When children play hide-and-seek, they may think they are well hidden, but their dog can find them right away. The same is true when a child is lost or wanders away from home. Aero can find the child by using his sense of smell. Each person has a scent that is different from everyone else's scent. Even twins do not smell the same. A person's unique smell comes from the food he or she eats, the soap and shampoo he or she uses, the clothes he or she wears, and the place he or she lives.

sense of smell

Aero has been trained and certified to find illegal drugs. He never needs to see the drugs to find them. His nose leads him right to the hiding place. He will then go on "alert" to let Officer Mike know where the drugs are hidden. He will bark and scratch at the hiding place. Officer Mike is trained to understand Aero's actions. Aero will earn a special reward—he gets to chase his tennis ball.

Aero has many friends at the fire station and often visits them with Officer Mike. Sometimes the firefighters have a pizza. When people smell pizza, they smell a delicious treat. But Aero, with his powerful nose, can

smell each item on the pizza separately. He can smell the cheese, the pepperoni, the mushrooms, the sausage, and the tomatoes.

Officer Mike and Aero work with the firefighters, too. When the firefighters answer an alarm, a police car always follows the fire truck or rescue squad. And when the S.W.A.T. team goes out, a paramedic firefighter always goes with them in case someone gets hurt. The two teams work together and help each other.

teamwork

at the vet's

Aero goes to Dr. Morse, a veterinarian, for regular checkups. Aero must lie still on a table while the doctor examines him. Once Aero had a small infection on his neck. Dr. Morse gave him some medicine so he would get better. Because a police dog works so hard and has such an important job, he needs to be healthy. At the end of the checkup, Dr. Morse lifts Aero to the floor, pets him, and says, "Good dog."

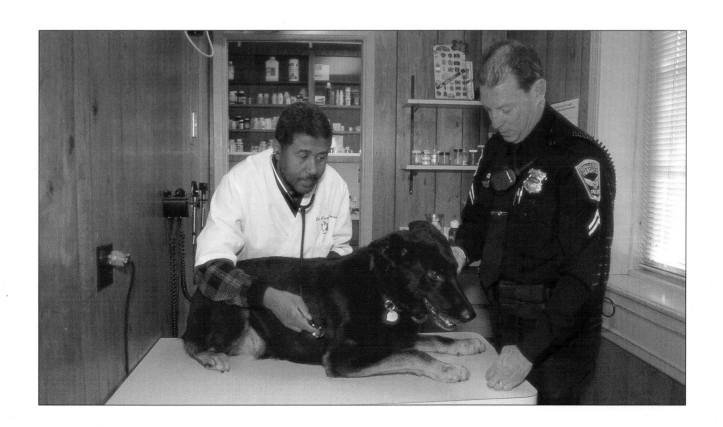

Nurses and teachers often write to the chief of police to ask if Aero can visit children in their hospital or their school. Aero likes children and is always gentle with them. He is even gentler when visiting a sick child. He lies down, staying very still and quiet so the child won't be afraid of him.

When Officer Mike and Aero visit schools, Aero rests on the floor beside Officer Mike. Together they demonstrate the different commands Aero will obey. The children ask many questions. Why is there a police badge on Aero's collar? How high can Aero jump? How fast can Aero run?

visiting in the

Officer Mike carefully answers the questions. Aero's badge shows everyone he is a working police dog. He can jump over an eight-foot wall when he is chasing a criminal. He can run very fast, about forty miles an hour. Even the fastest person can run only about twenty-four miles an hour.

Sometimes children ask Officer Mike about his gun. He tells them he never takes his gun out to show people. He takes it out only when he is on duty and needs to use it for his job or when he is at target practice.

community

Children often want to pet Aero. Officer Mike tells them the rules. Never try to pet a strange dog until you ask permission from the owner. Never come up behind Aero; he might get frightened and snap at you. Never ever hug a K-9 around the neck. Walk up to a police dog slowly from the front so he can see you. Let him sniff your hand. Pet his head and ears gently. Talk to him softly.

At the end of a twelve-hour work shift, there is always a final job to be done at the police station. After talking with his friends on the force, Officer Mike sits down and writes a report for the police chief about the whole day or night. Aero lies down by Officer Mike's chair. Maybe he's dreaming about his next meal or hoping Officer Mike will change into sweatpants so they can take a long run by the lake.

back at the station

After the report is written, Officer Mike and Aero go home together and have a meal with Officer Mike's wife and daughter and Tarzan and Zeus.

When Officer Mike takes a shower, Aero follows him into the bathroom and stays by the tub. Aero is always there to protect his partner. When Officer Mike goes to bed, Aero will plop down on the floor near the bed, lay his head on his paws, and with a sigh go to sleep near his best friend. Neither of them knows what surprises tomorrow's patrol will bring, but they are well prepared. They both love being police officers.

fellow officers

tools for the job

badge with state seal

hat with waterproof brim

patrolman's formal uniform

radio microphone

police badge

bulletproof vest (always worn under uniform)

pens

city police patch

S.W.A.T. pin

accreditation pin

K-9 handler pin

pad with waterproof paper (in pocket)

corporal stripes

name tag

years of service pin

radio controls

also on Officer Mike's utility belt:

gun

collapsible baton
handcuffs

gun belt and holster

pepper spray

remote car-door opener

bullets

Aero's leash

alert mind

watchful eyes

acute hearing

keen sense of smell

leather work collar with police badge

strong jaws and sharp teeth

rabies vaccination tag

quiet paws

powerful muscles and strong legs

work boots